Old Aspatria

by Trevor Grahamslaw

Aspatria Agricultural College RUFC 1913-14, left to right top row - M D Wilson, F S Scott, F Adams, W E Prentice, W Fanning, H C Webb, R Somers Cocks. Middle Row - A H Hyams, A W L Smith, R Lawton Roberts (Capt), H F H Barber, T Worth. Seated F H Crowe, G M K Young, E J C Vint. Recreational activities were encouraged with the college fielding rugby, football, cricket, athletics and tennis teams on nearby Beacon Hill fields, whilst drama, dances and reunions of the "Old Aspatrian Club" (consisting of former students) were held at the Market Hall. However, this poignant 1914 photograph marked the end of an era. By August most of the students had enlisted to fight in the First World War (1914-18) and college pupil numbers declined. In 1925 the principal, J Smith – Hill, closed the college, which was demolished in 1953 and replaced by Beacon Hill School in 1965.

Aspatria Agricultural College July 1914 left to right, top row - E M K Young, F Adams, F H Crowe, W Prentice, F S Scott, W Fanning, Bowcher. Middle row - H Gilleat, H C Webb, E F Twelves Taylor, Wilson, J Bullen, R Sowers, Cox, Darwell, Lewis, E J C Vint. Front row - R Lawton-Roberts, H Barber, C Charleton, J Robinson (lecturer), J Smith-Hill (principal), Henry Thompson (vet), A H Hymes, A W L Smith. Dr H J Webb died in January 1894 being succeeded by J Smith-Hill whose curriculum of practical scientific farming, improved stock breeding and land utilisation techniques, together with a butter quality research programme in partnership with the West Cumberland Dairy Company trained specialist graduates as land agents and for senior agricultural posts abroad.

Acknowledgements

For help in compiling this book the author would like to thank: First Milk, Duncan Hillary of Aspatria Farmers Ltd, Dennis Perriam, Wendy Campbell, Ernie Ridley, Billy McMurray, Bill and Olga Reid, Billy Bouch, and particularly Anne Usher Thomas and John Symn for there support and encouragement.

Picture Acknowledgements

Anne Usher Thomas: 5, 8, 21, 26, 33, 37, 38, 41, 45, back cover.
Bill & Olga Reid: 6, 13, 36, 48.
Muriel Bouch: 15.
John Symn: 20, 22, 27, 28.
Joan Graham: 23.
Sean Bell of First Milk: 25.
Eric Reynolds: 32.
Johnny Elliott: 39.
Christine Harrison for Aspatria Bowling Club: 43.
George Johnston: 44.
Linda Snowden: Inside front cover.

Further Reading

John Rose & Margaret Dunglinson, *Aspatria*, Phillimore, 1987

Anne Usher Thomas, *Aspatria*, Alan Sutton Publishing, 1993

Oliver Wood, *West Cumberland Coal*, Cumberland & Westmorland Antiquarian & Archaeological Society, 1988.

Text © Trevor Grahamslaw, 2009.
First published in the United Kingdom, 2009,
by Stenlake Publishing Ltd.
Telephone: 01290 551122
www.stenlake.co.uk

ISBN 9781840334838

Introduction

In 1843 the Maryport & Carlisle Railway Company laid the last rail connecting Carlisle to the coast. Aspatria was merely a request stop, but in common with most Cumberland villages the residents were fiercely proud of their town and dialect, persuading the train guards to announce "Spatry loup oot" as the train approached the platform. Today the dialect persists with the "Spatry" accent proclaiming the unique character of this historic village.

The first settlers in the region were Mesolithic hunter-gatherers around 5000BC, followed some 3,000 years later by Neolithic farmers who cultivated the land below the hills that form Aspatria's backbone. From around 300BC the Brigantes tribe colonised the area, until AD71 when it was subjugated by the Romans. With no strategic value, Aspatria did not merit a fort, being merely a hamlet on the Roman military road between the forts at Olenacum (Old Carlisle) and Alauna (Maryport). With the collapse of the Roman Empire, around AD383, the area was abandoned as Britain entered the Dark Ages. By the fifth century the Christian Celtic Kingdom of Rheged ruled north-west England with Christian missionaries spreading the gospel. Saint Ninian, born in AD360, who preached throughout Rheged, was followed by Saint Patrick, born AD387, who may be the root of Aspatria's name - "the ash tree or grove of Patrick" in Norse. But the most influential saint was Kentigern (also known as Mungo). Born in AD518, Kentigern was elected first bishop of Glasgow in AD543, but was forced out of Strathclyde by invading pagan tribes. As he moved south, preaching Christianity, believers dedicated their churches to him, including Aspatria, until he finally found sanctuary in Wales. After defeat at the battle of Chester in AD615, Rheged was overrun by the Anglian empire and settled by Norse migrants who reached Aspatria around AD950. Viking artefacts, including a hogback tombstone and crucifix shaft, survive in St Kentigern's Church. A dagger, sword, shield and clothing of a seven foot tall man excavated from a Beacon Hill barrow (tomb) in 1789 by Aspatria surgeon Mr Rigg, are in the British Museum. Two years after the Norman Conquest of England in 1066, the Solway Plain was part of Scotland, but in 1092 King William II seized Carlisle, appointing Ranulph de Meschines as grantee of Cumberland. The Manor of Aspatria was in turn granted by Ranulph to Waltheof, Lord of Allerdale, with Waltheof's son Alan giving the small Manor of Brayton and Oughterside to Ughtred from Oughterside. Scotland's claim to Cumberland continued and although Scottish reivers rarely raided as far south as Allerdale, Aspatria men did their share of manning the Border Watch. The Union of the English and Scottish Crowns in 1603 brought relative stability to the Solway Plain as Aspatria's population of 180 worked the nine farmsteads straggling the former Roman Road (now King Street and Queen Street). By 1801 Aspatria's population was made up of 106 families of 327 people, inhabiting 98 houses, rising to 478 people by 1812 when Wilfrid Wyburgh Lawson became the first Baronet of Brayton.

It remained an agricultural hamlet until the discovery of a rich coal seam in the 1850s and Joseph Harris and Wilfrid Lawson sank the first mines. The influx of Scottish and Irish labourers would swell Aspatria's population to over 3400 by the time Brayton Domain No 5 pit opened in 1912. With industrial prosperity and the arrival of the railway Aspatria blossomed. The Agricultural Co-operative Society was formed in 1870, The Market Hall opened in 1872, the Agricultural College in 1874, Aspatria Rugby Club was founded in 1879, the Reading Room and Library opened in 1894 and Richmond Hill School in 1895. All this was overseen by Wilfrid Lawson, MP, whose radical Liberal views and, much to the dismay of Aspatria's publicans, support for temperance, earned him the title "Wilberforce of the Drink Traffic". Coal mining ended in 1942, but Aspatria's continued prosperity came through diversity - the Milk Marketing Board's Creamery in 1934, Larma Ltd (clothing manufacturer) in 1945 and the bed manufacturer M Hackney & Co (now Sealy) in 1947. There were also new housing estates at St Mungo's Park (1921), Noble Croft (1937), North View (1950), Brayton Park (1965), Harriston New Village (1973) and Sheila Fell Close in 2008. Sheila Fell R.A. (1931-1979), daughter of Anne and miner Jack Fell of 69 Queen Street, was a close friend of the artist L.S Lowry, who paid her a weekly allowance to buy art materials, and accompanied her on summer painting trips around Aspatria. These visits resulted in many of Sheila's finest landscape paintings, as she remembered her Aspatria childhood whilst working. In her own words; "I can remember watching the miners strung along the road, or crouching at Walter Wilson's corner with bait boxes ... farm carts full of hay and turnips ... then in the soft, black evenings, when the lights would glow from the houses, everything silent" - "Cumberland is not like the rest of England. It is like no other place". Today Aspatria remains, at heart, the pit village remembered by Sheila Fell. Colliers no longer walk the long streets and most of the small family shops have closed, but "Spatry" has retained its identity, pride in its rugby team, tight family connections and, above all, its distinctive character.

Agricultural College, Aspatria.

Aspatria Agricultural College School, Beacon House on Market Square, around 1900. Following the success of the 1870 founded Aspatria Agricultural Co-operative Society, two of its directors, William Norman (b.1839) and John Twentyman (b.1840) with a number of associates, including Wilfrid Lawson of Brayton Hall as president, opened the college in 1874. It was not a success, due to the low number of student applications, and when Dr H J Webb took over in 1885, had debts exceeding £2,000. He secured a government grant, cleared the debt, and in 1893 bought adjacent land, and engaged the Carlisle architect, Taylor Scott to increase the dormitory accommodation to 65 students. He taught scientific and practical farming.

Paying Mr Ellwood £100 for the ground, the Aspatria Public Hall Company Ltd was founded in 1872 for the specific purpose of raising the finance to build the Market Hall and Assembly Rooms in Market Place. The plans were prepared by a Mr Eaglesfield and the construction carried out by a Mr Crosthwaite – with the clock bought from its manufacturer, Mr C Stonehouse, for £75. By the 1930s it had fallen into disuse and was bought by Thomas Ostle (1874-1953), who re-opened it as a furniture saleroom, the occasional meeting room and, as with many other halls at this time, a roller skating rink, managed by Charlie Over of the cinema. When skating rolled out of fashion in the late 1940s, Ostle sold it to the Ministry of Labour for a Labour Exchange. Today (2009) it is occupied by *Brownz Total Fitness*.

The day prior to Sir Wilfrid Lawson's funeral on 4 July 1906, a meeting in the Market Hall resolved to open a subscription fund to erect a memorial water fountain to his memory. Over £1,100 was raised and the Manchester based sculptor, Louis Fritz Roselieb *alias* Louis Frederick Roslyn was commissioned. Working with Messrs Kirkpatrick, he designed this 24 feet Derbyshire granite pedestal, topped with St George slaying the dragon and three bronze panels depicting a likeness of Sir Wilfred, classically attired women offering water to a traveller and a Roman soldier clasping the hand of the barbarian. The site was donated by the agricultural college. It was unveiled by Sir Josslyn Francis Pennington (1834-1917), 5th Baron Muncaster, then Lord Lieutenant of Cumberland, on 21 April 1908, drinking its first beaker of water to the cause of temperance. Roslyn later sculpted a statue of Sir Wilfred for London's Victoria Embankment Gardens.

1930s Aspatria Market Place. Behind the Lawson Monument are Over & Sons' petrol pumps and the District Bank Chambers - the Westminster Bank from 1968 and now (2009) the Natwest bank. On the right is Castle Terrace, and the Aspatria Volunteer Fire Brigade's depot, having moved here in 1905 from its original engine shed, built 1874, beside the King Street Co-op, and bringing the stone plaque "Fire Brigade Depot 1874". In 1947 the Brigade became part of the Cumberland Fire Service moving in the 1950s to their current King Street location. Next right is Martha Bouch the grocer and next again, Mary Bouch the stationer. In 1878 Cephas Bouch opened a newsagent and tobacconist here and his great grandsons continue to trade, with Kevin at no. 12 as a general store and newsagent, and Billy as a grocer at 26 King Street.

Long before the Lawson Memorial drinking fountain, Market Place was known as Brandreth Green, with a pond, the Brandreth Pot, beside the village green - a popular stop for travellers to water their horses. The wagon on the left, under the Market Hall tower, would be an itinerant trader or showman. Beyond, are the Bank Chambers then Castle Terrace with St Kentigern's Church tower on the horizon. Opposite, are the fire station, Bouch's grocery shop, a former blacksmiths workshop, the Grapes Hotel and Henry Thompson's veterinary practice at Beacon View House. In the centre stands the "Bray Lamp" erected by Aspatria Local Board in 1893 - Market Place's only illumination.

The veterinary surgeon Henry Thompson (born at Allonby in 1836, died 1920), wearing the panama hat, and his son Charles, in the doorway of their home and surgery, Beacon View House, in Market Place. In 1869 local farmers John Twentyman of Hawkrigg Farm and William Norman of High Close, Aspatria, supported by Wilfrid Lawson (Brayton Hall) and his brother William Lawson, Mechi Farm, Blennerhasset, dissatisfied with the cost, and quality, of available manure, took action, and at a meeting in the Grapes Hotel on 24 January 1870 founded the Aspatria Agricultural Co-operative Society - the county's first farmers' co-operative. The 20 members purchased £1 subscription shares and Henry Thompson became its secretary, serving until his death in 1920, on an initial salary of £65 per annum. He was provided with an office and warehouse in West Street and tasked with guaranteeing the quality of feeding stuffs and fertilizers.

Market Square in the 1920s, when Herbert Swetland was landlord of the newly renovated Grapes Hotel – the work having included an additional third storey. Next is Beacon View, home of Henry Thompson, bought in the 1930s by Doctor Archibald Kilmorack Rankins, for his surgery. Beyond is Station Road then John Tweedle's Brandraw Hotel, and through the trees can be glimpsed the 1879 built Brandraw House.

LAWSON STREET
ASPATRIA

The westward view along Lawson Street in the 1900s. Built between 1855 and 1885, partly by Brayton Domain Collieries and partly by individuals, Lawson Street stretches from Park Road West to the Brewery Corner junction (after Benjamin Kendall's brewery which closed in 1883) to join Brayton Road and Queen Street. On the left is the entrance to the Aspatria Gas & Light Company's gas works, founded in 1859 with a share capital of £6000. The works were partly financed by Wilfrid Lawson, who installed gas lighting (and gas powered heating in the Brayton Estate glasshouses) at Brayton Hall, whilst Aspatria became one of the first towns in Cumberland with street gas lighting.

The Wesleyan Chapel on the corner, as North Road turns into Queen Street, in the 1900s. It was built in 1896, but demolished and replaced by a larger chapel in 1929, the Wesleyans using the Industrial Co-operative Hall in King Street in the interim. In June 2000, Aspatria Town Council and the Friends of Sheila Fell dedicated a slate plaque on the chapel wall to the town's most famous daughter, the landscape painter Sheila Fell RA, one of the finest British landscape painters of the 20th Century. On the right is Croft House and Thomas Watson the grocer.

QUEEN STREET, ASPATRIA.

10792

Running east, King Street and this part of Queen Street follow the Roman Road connecting the forts of Alauna (Maryport), Papcastle (Derventio) and Olerica (Blennerhasset) with Olenacum (Old Carlisle). This 1950s photograph shows how commercial Queen Street then was. On the left, the first awning shades the premises of G Richards the draper, whilst the second covers Tinnon Brothers, the electrical engineers. Further along J W Mathews, baker, and Joseph Pattinson the chemist are also in the shade.

QUEEN ST. ASPATRIA.

In 1909 you could buy anything and everything in Queen Street. The children with pram are outside Daniel Wilson, the watchmaker, with, further along the Misses Frances & Martha Brough, dressmakers; Thomas Ferguson, draper; William Hodgson the painter and decorator; Arthur Oliver, grocer; Jacob Young, fruiterer; William Young, furniture dealer; James G Bell, mineral water manufacturer, and Robert James Forester, the grocer. Opposite, was Joseph Askew the stationer and William Tate the clogger.

Queen Street, looking west, with Walter Wilson's grocery store on the junction with Harriston Road, on the left, and the fishmonger Thomas Rayner and Isaac Allen's general store opposite. In the far distance, where the road rises beside the trees, is Linden House. Like Yarra House, on King Street, it was a boarding school adopted by Aspatria Agricultural College in the 1870s to lodge students.

Thomas Watson (b. 1856) and his wife Betsy (b. 1854) flank one of their sons in the doorway of their 1889 established grocer's shop at 18 Queen Street in 1909. Four of their employees, including Daniel Hetherington, on the right of the group, stand to the left. He would open a baker's shop, at 85 King Street, after the First World War. The entry on the left led to a warehouse and granary, and the Watsons lived at Croft House, to the right of the shop. The premises are now (2009) occupied by a Spar supermarket.

St Kentigern (518-603) was exiled from Strathclyde by pagan Norse invaders shortly after becoming the first bishop of Glasgow in 543 and, travelling south, preached at Aspatria's Saxon church before going on to Wales. Around 1100 this Saxon church, now named Saint Kentigern's, was replaced by a Norman style church, which in 1848, was rebuilt in the Victorian Gothic style we see today. A salvaged Norman arch was incorporated in the vestry doorway, and the font, removed during the Reformation, was retrieved from the churchyard, repaired and returned to the church together with Scandinavian stone crosses and hogback tombstones. In 1875 Sarah Langcake, 2 King Street, donated £200 for an organ, the £40 tower clock was given by Rebecca Powell in memory of her husband, the Reverend Thomas Wade Powell (vicar 1879-1885), and in 1898 a public subscription purchased the tower's peal of eight bells – refurbished and re-dedicated in 1999. In the churchyard is St Kentigern's Well where early Christians were baptised.

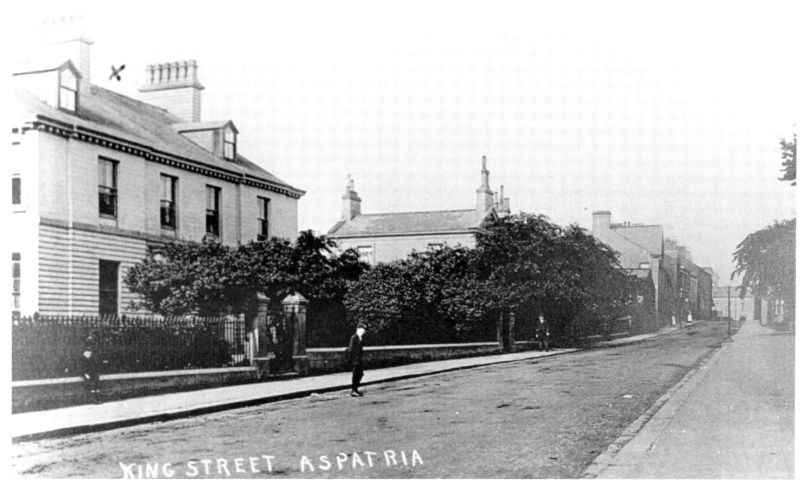

KING STREET ASPATRIA

King Street looking east with the Regency period Yarra House on the left, built by the first baronet of Brayton, Sir Wilfrid Lawson (1795-1867) as a girls' boarding school in 1820. With classrooms downstairs, the students' dormitories and teachers' quarters on the first floor and the servants' rooms in the attics, it had stables and a tennis court to the rear. It was bought by Aspatria Agricultural College in the 1870s for student accommodation. A Grade 2 listed building, today it is a private residence. Behind the trees is Springwell House, built in the 1890s.

Children play hopscotch outside a branch of the Carlisle Steam Laundry on Castle Terrace in 1924. Founded in 1890, it had its head office at Warwick Road, Carlisle but closed down in 1948. Opposite are the reading rooms of the Aspatria Reading & Recreation Co Ltd, established in 1889 with initial capital of 1,000, £1 shares, half taken by Lady Mary Lawson wife of the second baronet of Brayton Wilfrid Lawson, the building being erected in 1894. On the ground floor it had a reading room, two bathrooms, games, smoking and committee rooms and a caretaker's apartment, whilst upstairs were two billiard tables and the library. In 1940 the library, then downstairs, was bought by Aspatria Town Council, whilst the Aspatria Reading & Recreation Co Ltd folded in 1948 due to declining membership.

CASTLE TERRACE.

John Ridley, postmaster, confectioner and china dealer's shop at 5 King Street, and the red sandstone built Castle Terrace in the 1900s. It is little changed today (2009) with even the railings removed during the Second World War having been replaced, although slate roofs have been added to most of the bay windows.

Jack and Fred Symn, with their father Joseph outside their drapery shop (Joseph Symn's, established 1902) at 10a and 12a King Street, opposite Castle Terrace, in the 1930s. Jack married Madge Barber, the daughter of Francis Penrice Barber, headmaster of Hayton School (near Aspatria), whilst Fred married Dorothy Dial who eventually ran H L Dial's grocer's shop in Station Road. In the 1930s the trading name was changed from Joseph Symn's to Symns, and closed in 1965. It is now (2009) occupied by Castle Financial Services.

Left: Joseph Pattinson served his apprenticeship with William Sparks, who had opened a chemist shop at 43 Queen Street in 1894, and when Sparks retired, Pattinson bought the business and moved it to 48 King Street, pictured here. By 1910 Pattinson would move again, to 56 King Street, adjoining Springwell House. In the 1930s Joseph retired and his son Eric took over the business, buying Maurice Litt's chemist shop at 61 Queen Street. Between 1934 and 1948 they had a chemist van, touring neighbouring villages and manned by Andrew Douglas and Tom Routledge. In 1957 Eric retired, closing the King Street shop and selling the business at 61 Queen Street to Raymond Southgate, who closed it in 1960.

Right: King Street in the 1900s. From the left, is the wall of St Kentigern's Church, the lane leading to the vicarage, and a confectioner's shop which became George Goodhall's plumbers by 1910, and Daniel Hetherington's bakery by 1921. Next is Daniel Crossthwaite, the clogger and then the Fox & Hounds Inn (formerly the Hare and Hounds) with landlord Joseph Mumberson. By 1910 Joseph had left the Fox & Hounds for the Vaults (later the Letters Inn) on Outgang Road.

Jim N Over, jeweller, watch repairer, optician and cycle dealer, standing outside his King Street shop in the 1930s. This entrance to the premises was in the lane connecting King Street (on the left) with Outgang Road. The posters at the shop corner advertise films showing at the Queen's Hall Picture Palace across the road from where Jim stands. Originally built of wood by the Biddalls, a circus family, in 1911, it was bought by Jim's father Charlie Over and rebuilt in brick in 1939. When Charlie died in 1948 the cinema was managed by Jim with his niece Ella. In 1983 following a major fire, it reopened as the Palace Bingo Hall. In 2003 Ella Over closed the Palace, and it was demolished in 2007. The site was developed in 2008 into new houses named Overs Court.

Sam Arnott in the doorway of *The Vaults Inn* on Outgang Road in the early 1940s, after taking over from Jane Elizabeth Moore. Within a few years Sam would change the name to *The Letters Inn*. In the yard is Tom 'Tykes' Little's grocery cart. Tykes, who lived in a cottage at Hallbank Farm, sold fruit and vegetables around the district and had probably stopped for refreshment before driving out to Westnewton village.

WEST STREET, ASPATRIA.

West Street, looking east towards Market Place in the 1900s. On the right is the West Street pond, drained in the 1940s when the wall was straightened in line with the road. Today only a remnant of the pond remains, as part of a small nature reserve maintained by pupils of Beacon Hill School.

The Dairy Crest creamery, Station Road in 1972, two years before its refurbishment. From the left, is the cheese store warehouse, the engineer's workshop, the boiler house with its chimneys, the cheese press buildings and the packing rooms - with Station Road running behind. The first creamery was built on Station Road in 1888 by the West Cumberland Dairy Company, in co-operation with the Aspatria Agricultural Co-operative Society, on land leased from Sir Wilfrid Lawson. However, within a few years, it was taken over by Messrs Carrick of Newcastle and closed in 1924. In 1934 the Milk Marketing Board – trading as Dairy Crest – renovated the works and operated it as their first cheese-producing factory. The 1974 revamp increased the processing capacity to 500,000 litres of milk a day. First Milk, the UK's largest dairy co-operative and cheese maker, acquired the company in 2006.

A 1900s photograph of a soldier and child walking towards Comely Bank – joined to Aspatria by Station Road in 1845, when the railway station opened – with Ferguson the coach builder's, founded by John Ferguson in the 1850s to build horse-drawn carriages, premises on the left. An apprentice, William Casson (b.1844), later joined Hooper & Son of London, where he designed the Casson two wheel brake in 1880, and bespoke carriages for European and American customers. In 1890 he was awarded the Freedom of the Worshipful Company of Coach & Harness Makers and later became a Freeman of the City of London. In 1901 John Ferguson's son Thomas sold the business to A Ross & Sons who traded until the First World War (1914-1918). On the right, below St Kentigern's tower, is Joseph Hillary's Agricultural Engineering and Millwright Works.

"Baden" Holliday, Alfie Foster, Fred Barwise and Tom Nelson in front of Joseph Dial's lorry loaded with a hay bale transporter from Joseph Hillary, the agricultural implement maker on Station Road, in 1936. They are outside Helen Lucy Dial's (wife of Henry Dial and mother of Joseph and Dorothy Dial) grocery shop at 6 Station Road, the business having been started in the front room of Helen and Henry's house at 2 Station Road in the 1890s and moved to these premises in 1912. On her death in 1946 the business passed to Dorothy or Dorrie (1900-1996) who married Fred Symn closing the shop on retiral in 1982.

Standing with a Lewis, single cylinder, diesel powered milking machine at Joseph Hillary's Agricultural Engineering and Millwright Works on Station Road in 1926, are, left to right: Edward Hillary, son of Joseph Hillery, 31 Arkleby Road; William Yeowart, fitter, 91 King Street; Joseph Hillary, the firm's founder, millwright and former mining fitter, 49 Arkleby Road, and Fred Barwise, blacksmith, from Mealrigg. In the late 1990s Joseph's grandson Tom Hillary retired and his sons Duncan and Martin took over the business. However, Martin left, and in 2006 the economic uncertainty in farming led Duncan to sell the company to Aspatria Farmers Ltd, formed in the late 1980s from the 1870 founded Aspatria Agricultural Co-operative Society, enabling them to offer a full range of farm supplies - from feed to machinery.

Looking from Aspatria railway station west. On the left is the siding for the Bolton Loop line opened in 1866 (from Aspatria through Boltons Parish to Aikbank Junction) to collect coal from Allhallows Colliery at Mealsgate. The footbridge was erected in the 1890s, the only other crossing being down steps either side of the track from Bower Bridge behind. Further right is a water trough then the station office with Ferguson Coach Builder's Workshop beyond on Station Road. The Maryport & Carlisle Railway Company line from Maryport to Arkleby Pit opened in 1840, by 12 April 1841 it reached Aspatria and in 1843 joined the Carlisle line at Wigton. Constructed to move coal and coke to Maryport Dock or by rail to the Workington and Lanarkshire steelworks, by 1888 the railway was also transporting tankers of fresh milk from the West Cumberland Dairy Company to London. Today Aspatria is a request stop on the Northern Rail line from Carlisle to Barrow in Furness.

The Maryport & Carlisle Company's locomotive, Number 8, a 2-4-0, built at their works at Grasslot, Maryport in 1876, at Aspatria Station, photographed before World War One from the Bower Bridge. The soldiers would have been of the Territorial Army (formed 1908) going to Workington for training. On the left are the water trough and the main station buildings, whilst to the far right is the West Cumberland Dairy Company works.

The western view of Brayton Hall House with cattle grazing in parkland landscaped by the 10th Baronet, Sir Wilfrid Wyburgh Lawson. The Hall was built of red freestone, painted white, with a Grecian style colonnade entrance of Prudhoe white stone. The first recorded owner of Brayton was Alan, second Lord of Allerdale (b. 1106), who granted it to Ughtred from Uchtredby (Oughterside) about 1143, who changed his name to Brayton. It passed to the Bewley family, and in 1572 was acquired by the Salkelds. In 1658 the estate was sold by three Salkeld co-heiressess for £1000 to the Lawson family, who also owned the Isel and Hesket estates. In 1806 Sir Wilfrid Wyburgh Lawson (b. 1764), the 10th Baronet of Brayton & Isel, died and the estate passed to his wife's nephew Thomas Wybergh. Upon Thomas's death in 1812 the estate passed to his brother Wilfrid (1795-1867) who assumed the name Lawson and was made first baronet of Brayton. He was succeeded by his son Wilfrid (1829-1906) as second baronet, then his grandson Wilfrid (1862-1937) as third baronet, and finally the second baronets grandson Hilton (1895-1959) who died unmarried leaving no direct heir to the baronetcy.

During the early 19th century Brayton Hall was improved by Sir Wilfrid Wyburgh Lawson, Bart (1795-1867), with extensions added to the western and southern wings. The Hall now boasted an entrance hall, drawing room, morning room, dining room, billiard room, library, smoking room, schoolroom and seventeen bedrooms. There were also fourteen servant's bedrooms, domestic offices, a gunroom, game larder and laundry. This 1880s photograph of the south wing, shows this Georgian style mansion with plaque (above the windows) topped by the Lawson crest – two arms embowed, vested argent (silvery-white), representing the arms of the law, supporting a sun in splendour. The crest was a pun on the name Law-son. On the right is the schoolroom and in front a sunken garden divided from the parkland by a small stream. At 10.00am on 21 September 1918 a fire lit to air the drawing room, fanned by a southerly wind, spread. The Aspatria Fire Brigade arrived but was only able to use mains water, as Brayton Pond proved insufficient. By 1.00pm the Workington motor fire engine became mired in muddy ground and took hours to free. By 2.00am the following morning the fire was out leaving the west front and part of the south wing gutted and the schoolroom and north wing damaged. Plans to rebuild the Hall were never completed, with the Lawson family moving to Isel Hall on 22 September 1924. Abandoned, the Hall quickly became ruinous.

An 1890s photograph of the ivy clad Jubilee Lodge, erected at the southern entrance to the Brayton Estate in 1887, to commemorate Queen Victoria's Golden Jubilee. The previous cottage on the site was home to the estate gamekeeper, John Husband (1845-1890), until the first Sunday in February 1870, when the flue from the kitchen fireplace became blocked and fire broke into an upstairs bedroom. John and his mother escaped moments before the fire ignited a chest of gunpowder stored in the bedroom, blowing the lodge's roof off. Despite Sir Wilfrid's best hunting guns being destroyed, John was kept on as gamekeeper, eventually being re-housed in an estate cottage at Wellington Farm. The plaque of three scrolled letters above the window are; L (Lawson), W (Wilfrid) and M (Mary).

Wilfrid Lawson's West Cumberland Foxhounds gather beside the Station Lodge entrance to the estate, but without Wilfrid, in 1906. Wilfrid Lawson was a huntsman like John Peel (1777-1854) hunting with him in the Northern Fells around Aspatria, preventing foxes preying on sheep. They were unlikely companions, Peel being a hard-drinking, uneducated, fell farmer, whilst Lawson was teetotal, perhaps why the hunt master in the photograph may be drinking tea, cultured and noble, but their love of hunting made them firm friends. When Peel (immortalised in the song *D'ye ken John Peel*) died in 1854, Wilfrid amalgamated many of Peel's hounds into his own pack. Today the descendants of Lawson's pack, the Cumberland Foxhounds, are kennelled at Westward Park, Wigton. The Station Lodge, the road and the railway signal house at the road end were all built in 1845, after directors of the Maryport and Carlisle Railway Company resolved on 8 March 1845 that, "in consequence of the pecuniary assistance rendered by Sir Wilfrid Lawson ... all trains do stop to take up and put down, when a signal is displayed at a private signal house ... called Brayton Station".

Brayton Estate gardener's cottage, to the west of the Piscina (fishpond) and the cricket ground, and north of Brayton Tarn, in the 1900s. In 1941, Aspatria businessman, Dryden Ward, and his sons Dryden and Barrie, bought the estate. Their re-development included converting this cottage to the Lakeside Restaurant, opening a woodyard near Station Lodge, and laying out a members' golf course, extending from the restaurant, across the former cricket pitch to the ruins of Brayton Hall. The course remains popular today.

An election poster for Sir Wilfrid Lawson's Liberal campaign for Cockermouth in the 1906 General Election. He won his first parliamentary seat, Carlisle, in 1859 and represented the town until resigning in 1871, when a new parliamentary constituency was created at Cockermouth. He lost, but was elected six months later at a General Election and represented Cockermouth until 1903 when his anti-imperialism views on the Boer War (1899-1902) led to defeat. He contested, and won, Cambourne in Cornwall in the 1903 election but resigned in 1906 to contest Cockermouth in the February, which he won again. He died on 1 July 1906. He was an untiring reformer, supporting electoral reform, Irish Home Rule, and the abolition of alcoholic drink. He was also a founder member of Aspatria Agricultural College and chairman of the Carlisle & Maryport Railway Co (1874-1906). He married Mary Pocklington Senhouse (b.1839), the daughter of Joseph Pocklington Senhouse Esq of Netherhall, at St Mary's Church, Maryport on 13 November 1860, and had 8 children - Wilfrid, Ellen, Arthur, Mordaunt, Mabel, Lucy, Josephine and Godfrey.

In the western garden of Brayton Hallare is the palm house built by Sir Wilfrid Lawson (1795-1867) as an improvement to the estate. Following the founding of the Aspatria Gas & Light Company Limited on Lawson Street in 1859, gas was piped to Brayton Hall, to light the house and heat the palm house, permitting the cultivation of out of season fruit and vegetables. Lawson was a member of the 1835 founded British Association for the Promotion of Temperance and in 1839 emptied the contents of his drinks cellar into the fishpond, earning it the sobriquet "The Whiskey Pond". His son, the second Baronet, also Wilfrid Lawson formed the National Temperance Movement in association with the Liberal Party in 1884 and actively campaigned to close many of Aspatria's pubs.

Left: Children and, perhaps, an elderly miner among the ruins of Brayton Domain No 3 pit (East Mill), whilst engineers work at the chimney base prior to its demolition, sometime after the pit's closure in October 1902. On the skyline are some of the 96 terraced cottages – Harris Town, later Harriston – built in the 1870s by mine owner Joseph Harris for his colliers at East Mill. Brayton Domain Colliery Company was founded in 1822 by Joseph Harris (1780- 1860) who already owned or leased collieries at Greysouthern, Maryport and Oughterside. His son John Harris (1827-1863) sank Brayton Domain No 1 pit, between the River Ellen and Aspatria Railway Station, in 1858. In 1863 Trustees acting for his son, Joseph Harris (1859-1946), opened Brayton Domain No 2, to the east of No 1. In August 1870 Brayton Domain No 3 pit was started on three acres of glebe land at East Mill, bought from St Kentigern's Church for £750.

Above right: Following on from the previous illustration the engineers, having removed sufficient brickwork at the base, supported the chimney with pit props, packed around with combustible material and set it alight. The props burnt through and the chimney came down. The Brayton Domain collieries followed the "Yard" seam, a band of rich bituminous coal, running from Whitehaven to Mealsgate, but the seam had faults, and Brayton No 1, opened in 1861, was worked out and closed in the 1870s. No 2, opened in 1863, was more successful becoming the most valuable coalfield in Cumberland at the time, extracting coal at 80 fathoms (480 feet) until meeting another fault in 1867, eventually closing in 1875. No 3 sunk into a 4 foot 9 inch seam in 1870, was worked until reaching another fault and closing in 1902. With the pit closed, the Harriston miners travelled a mile north to work at Brayton Domain No 4.

Brayton Domain No 4 (the Wellington Pit) shortly after its opening in 1888. On the left are the boiler house, its chimney, and the offices. Behind the offices on the right is the downcast main shaft with its larger headgear used to move men, materials and fresh air underground, next to the upcast shaft with smaller headgear for raising coal and expelling stale air from the mine. By 1890 coal was being raised 550 feet from the Yard Band and processed on site in coke ovens (east of this view) before being transported via the Maryport & Carlisle Railway (which passed behind the office buildings) to the Workington Steelworks, or the iron works in Lanarkshire. Some coal was also transported via the exchange siding at Brayton Station to the Solway Junction Railway for export from Silloth. A strike over the winter of 1932/33 resulted in No 4 flooding and, being almost worked out, never reopened. It closed officially on 24 March 1933 and was demolished in 1935.

Two miners working a Siskol coal cutter at the 600 feet level Yard Seam of No. 4 Brayton, photographed by Joseph Pattinson, the chemist and photographer of King Street, in 1910 – and one of a series he produced as postcards. Operating the machine is 54 year old Joseph Douglas. The Siskol Percussive Drill was powered by compressed air, controlled by the valve lever at Douglas's right hand, whilst his left hand operated the quadrant, which swung the machine into position to undercut the coal. The introduction of the Siskol drill reduced the hard labour of pick hewn coal.

Joseph Pattinson's photograph of Brayton Domain No 5. Left is the screens building where coal was hand picked to remove stone, then the main shaft and right the washery, capable of cleaning 70 tons of coal per hour. To the left of the chimney and boiler house, on the right, is the air shaft. No 5 was sunk beside the Maryport and Carlisle Railway line, west of Aspatria Station in 1907, and was the deepest of the Brayton pits, reaching the four foot thick Yard Seam at 1026 feet. Between 1913 and 1918 Brayton Domain No 4 and No 5 produced 200,000 tons of coal per annum. On 11 April 1942, with the seam at No 5 exhausted, the last Brayton pit closed.

The completion of the construction work on Brayton Domain No 5 pit in 1912 was marked by this photograph of colliery workers beside the main shaft. Miners, standing at the back, had an average working day of eight hours and a weekly pay of 7/1d, whilst surface workers and screen lassies (coal pickers), in the middle, earned 4/8. Boys, from fourteen years, also worked an eight hour, underground, shift, for around 2/- per week. Too young to cut coal, they controlled the ventilation doors, assisted the hewers, or carried coal baskets from narrow seams. The luckier ones drove the ponies on the trams collecting the coal. At this time over 500 people worked the Aspatria mines, many living in the purpose-built pit village of Harris Town, or in Aspatria.

OUGHTERSIDE COLLIERY

Oughterside Colliery in the early 1900s with the Maryport and Carlisle Railway Company siding and coal wagons being loaded from the overhead, and the headgear of the main shaft. The first record of an Oughterside pit dates from 1681, owned by William Orfeur of Plumbland. In 1753 the pits, formerly leased to William Fletcher of Moresby by the Duke of Somerset, were taken on by Wilfrid Lawson's co-heiresses, Elizabeth and Charlotte Lawson, but never worked. From 1814 to 1825 Brown Hodgson & Co leased them, losing £3000 due, in part, to the abundance of stone in the seam. But with the opening of the Maryport & Carlisle Railway in 1841, transport costs were cut and profitable mining became possible. In 1902 the colliery (pictured here), was owned by Hugh Cecil Lowther, 5th Earl of Lonsdale (1857-1944), and leased to the Oughterside Coal Co Ltd. They began raising coal in 1906 and had built 40, coke ovens on the site by 1913. The 1920s brought decline and closure came in 1933. Between 1936 and 1938 the Westmoor Colliery Co Ltd began extracting coal from a driftmine at Westmoor End until flooding ceased production. In 1939 the re-formed Oughterside Coal Co Ltd sank two shafts, Westmoor No 1 & No 2 into the Yard Seam, but output was poor and they were closed in 1943.

St Mungo's War Memorial Park from Outgang Road, shortly after its opening in February 1920. On the left, beyond the children's swings, is the Aspatria Recreation Bowling Club green with the tennis courts to the right. On the horizon are the houses of St Mungo's Park, built in a co-operative between North-Eastern Housing Association and Aspatria Urban District Council in 1921, having purchased most of the land from Thomas Ostle (1874-1953) of Outgang House, Aspatria. On the horizon is the tower of St Kentigern's Church.

Aspatria Bowling Club members at the presentation of a scoreboard by the bed manufacturers, Sealy UK (est. 1975) of Station Road in 1983. Front Row (left to right); David Bell, Eric Scaife, Horace Wreay, Dawson Sowerby, Tom Ashworth (senior), Gordon Young, Bobby Wood, Tom Peake, Gordon Stephenson, Stephen Cork, Jack Ashworth, John Wilkinson. Back Row; Tom Ashworth (junior), Tony Cork, Geff Pattinson, Cyril McDowell, Desmond Bell, John Bell, James Hodgson, Lenny Hodgson, Jobby Bell, Peter Pattinson, John Tremble, Bill Blackett, Mike Wilson. At the start of the 1986 season Sealy (UK) sponsored a new clubhouse opened by Wigton's bowling international, John Bell, and for a few years, used partly as a bed showroom.

Aspatria Colliery Silver Band, formed in the 1860s, outside the Market Hall in 1931. Front Row (left to right); R Tunstall, T Hewitson, John Willie Atkinson (conductor), W Atkinson, C Thompson, T Tunstall, G Graham and J Bell. Middle Row: H Graves, J W Glencross, W Robinson, J Ashworth, J Pearson, J Hewitson, W Robinson, I Maughan, J Wilkinson, J W Harker and G Benson. Back Row: Len Hewitson, G Robinson, J Thompson, T Ross, R Stoddart, Albert Mounsey, J Atkinson, J Cuthell, T Graves and G Bell. John Willie Atkinson (1882-1963), a miner for 45 years began playing in the Aspatria Fire Brigade Band as solo trombone in 1900, being promoted to conductor in 1914. In the 1920s the band amalgamated with the 5th Border Regiment Volunteer Band and was renamed the Colliery Band, until Brayton Domain No 5 Colliery closed in 1942. Re-formed as Aspatria Town Band it folded in 1967, the instruments being donated to Beacon Hill School.

Aspatria RUFC returning with the Cumberland Cup after beating Silloth, 20 points to 3 at Carlisle on 7 April 1909 – Joe Davidson having scored three tries, his brother George two conversions and a drop goal, and J Holliday one try. Part of the reception crowd was the Aspatria Fire Brigade Brass Band, seen with them here outside the Station Hotel. Founded in 1878, it was one of the seven founding members of the Cumberland County Rugby Football Union – with Carlisle, Eden Wanderers, Maryport, Workington, Whitehaven and Cockermouth, and won the inaugural Challenge Cup at Workington, beating Whitehaven by one goal to nil, and going on to win the Cup a record 31 times. They purchased Bower Park Field, off Station Road, in 1967, added a clubhouse in 1974 and built a grandstand in 1985.

Galas, coronation celebrations, bands and carnivals have paraded along Aspatria's streets over the centuries. This 1950s Carnival group at St Mungo's Park shows carnival characters in fancy dress ready for the judges. Among the characters, from left to right, are Richard Williams (Red Indian), Toby Irving (turning to camera), Thomas Watson (elf), Lena Brown, Edward Matthews (Cricketer), Ralph and Ann Irving (Groom & Bride), Harry Moore (behind Irving's with cap), Miss Mathews and Marian Mathews (ladies at back), Dorothy Towers (with cane), Audrey Towers (flower girl), Valerie Dixon (small child), Hilda Wilson (shawl), and Iris Armstrong (hat). It stopped in 1986 but was revived in 2000, and is once again one of the social highlights of the year, assembling at Aspatria Business Park, off Park Road, and parading through the town to Aspatria Rugby Club field.

As the new Brayton Domain mines prospered and miners' families moved into the area, schooling was needed for their children, so in 1875 Aspatria & Brayton School Board was founded. Initially, the 1825 built National School opposite St Kentigern's Church was enlarged in 1877, and then converted into a Sunday school when Richmond Hill School, with capacity for 650 pupils, was opened in 1895. This 1900s photograph of Richmond Hill's pupils, is without teachers or the headmaster, James Cobb – he famously guided his pupils through Brayton Hall during the fire of 1 September 1918, saving the library of 4,470 books, the pictures, furniture and china. In 1965 Richmond Hill became Aspatria's junior school, with the opening of Beacon Hill Secondary School, designed by Mr G K Seed and built on the site of former Aspatria Agricultural College.

John William Barnes, farmer, milkman and undertaker's assistant of Lawson Street, with William Hasting's (undertaker, Outgang Road) horse and hearse in Thomas Ostle's yard – where the hearse was garaged – on Outgang Road in 1945. Behind the horse, on the left, is the stone built engine house, which powered a circular saw, then the workshop, and on the right the woodstore with window. The two carts behind the hearse may have belonged to Ostle, or used in Hasting's secondary business as ashcarts. When horse-drawn hearses fell out of fashion a few years later, Hasting used this one as a greenhouse.